My Family Is Changing

My Family Is Changing

A Drawing and Activity Book for Kids of Divorce

Tracy McConaghie, LCSW, RPT/S

Illustrated by Karen Greenberg

ROCKRIDGE
PRESS

Dear Parents, Guardians, and Caregivers,

Divorce is challenging, and I know you want to support your child through this period of family change. As a child therapist for the past 25 years, I have had the joy of helping children make positive transitions through difficult times. This book is here to help your child identify their feelings and know those feelings are accepted and understood by the adults who care for them. That is the first step to moving through this time successfully.

The stories and activities in this book will help you and your child access, recognize, and express the feelings that accompany divorce. Through the stories here, your child will meet and relate to other children whose families are at various stages of the divorce process. Your child will learn about feelings and strategies for comfort and coping. In addition, they will read hopeful stories of children who have been through their parents' divorce and discovered they still have the love and stability they need.

I suggest you read through this book before sharing it with your child so that you will be prepared for their potential reactions and questions (and maybe for some of your own emotions as well). Reading and participating in the activities with your child can be a wonderful way to discover what they feel and need. With you as their guide, your child will also see that they are free to talk with you about their questions and concerns about your divorce.

If your child is a reader and wants some privacy, it is good to offer them that as well. You can let them know you have a book for them, and they can share their drawings and feelings with you if they choose. You can follow up with your child later and invite them to show you their work.

Working with this book may lead to important conversations between you and your child. The following guidelines will help you with those talks:

1. Some children ask "why" questions about the divorce, such as "Why are you getting a divorce?" or "Why can't you just get along?" It is important to give general answers rather than to share the specifics of your marriage difficulties. Keep in mind that a firm and positive attachment to both parents is essential. If children sense you are

hurt by or angry with their other parent, it will put them in an emotional dilemma that is an obstacle to their healing and well-being. Instead, share the general idea that sometimes parents find out they have grown-up problems that cannot be solved, or that they are happier if they work together as parents but are not married. This is sad for families, but they do get better and feel happy again.

2. Accept and allow any emotions your child shares. It is natural for parents to want to protect their children and make their hurts disappear. However, trying to smooth away the feelings of sadness, anger, disappointment, and worry is counterproductive. It inadvertently sends the message to your child that their feelings are not OK or that you cannot handle them. Instead, practice empathy and validation. Listen, be curious, and let them know it is OK to have feelings and to talk about them.

3. Your child may ask you a question you do not know the answer to, or one that you know the answer to but are not sure of the best way to respond. You may feel caught off guard and pressured to come up with something to say. Please remember this is a sensitive and difficult time, and it is OK to not know what to say. Take your time and tell your child that they have asked you a very important question. Explain that you need some time either to find out the answer or to think about the best way to explain the answer to them. Then you can consult with their other parent, trusted resources, or professionals so that you can respond thoughtfully when you are ready.

Divorce is sad and stressful, but families can and do recover if they are mindful of their children's needs and their own. It is natural for your child to show signs of stress for a little while, such as crying, behavior changes, mood changes, and difficulty sleeping. If these problems become a serious interference to family routine, school progress, or time with friends, consult with a professional therapist, preferably a play therapist who also specializes in families going through divorce.

I hope you find this book helpful, and I wish you and your family the very best on your journey to this next phase of your life.

Hi there!

I'm glad you have this new book. I wrote it just for kids like you whose parents are getting divorced.

There are children like you all over the world who understand how you're feeling. They have all kinds of feelings. They may be sad, happy, angry, or worried. Sometimes they feel more than one emotion at the same time. All of these feelings are totally OK.

This book will help you understand your feelings about your parents' divorce. Even though divorce is hard and your family is changing, there are people who love you and will take care of you. There are also things you can do to help yourself feel strong and calm.

You'll hear stories about children who are a lot like you, because their parents are getting divorced too. You'll also do some fun activities and drawings.

Let's get started!

Avi José Sarah Jin

Taylor Annabelle Nate

My name is Sarah. My parents just told me they're going
to get divorced and that soon our family will have two
homes instead of one. I used to hear my parents argue,
and sometimes that made me confused and scared. Now
I'm feeling very sad, and also worried. I don't know what
it will be like when my parents are divorced. There are so
many feelings inside of me!

Do you have a lot of feelings, too, like Sarah? Circle the faces that show what you feel about your parents' divorce. You can also use the empty circles to draw some of the other feelings you may have.

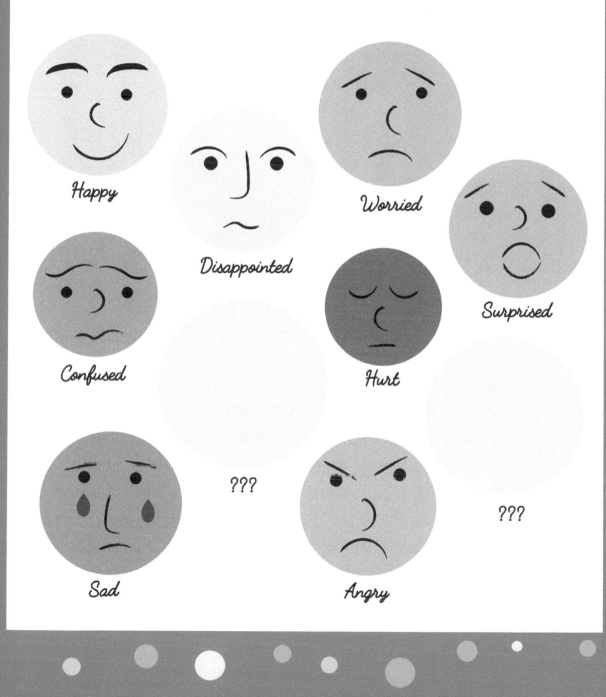

Happy

Disappointed

Worried

Surprised

Confused

Hurt

Sad

???

Angry

???

My teacher says it's important to pay attention to my feelings, even the hard ones. When I pay attention to how I'm feeling and take care of myself, I start to feel better. I can take care of myself by sitting quietly and breathing, getting a hug from someone who loves me, or snuggling my teddy bear. I also like to talk to my grandma, listen to my favorite music, and draw pictures of how I feel. What makes you feel comforted and calm?

This is your own wheel of comfort. In each section, draw something that helps you feel better. Maybe you get comfort from some of the same things that Sarah does, like a hug or a favorite stuffed animal. Or there may be different things that help you feel better.

My name is Nate. I'm in second grade, and I have a little sister. Now that my parents are getting divorced, we won't be able to see both of them every day. I think I'm going to miss them a lot when I'm not with them. I like it when my dad tucks me in at night, but now sometimes he won't be with me at bedtime.

Divorce is a change for your family. Some things will be different, and some will stay the same. Draw some things you think will be different in your family.

My parents explained to me that when I miss them,
I can talk to them on the phone, draw them a picture,
or tell my other parent how I'm feeling. I can also use the
things from my comfort wheel. My mom and dad said it's
important to remember that both of them love me and
will take care of me. I can feel their love even when we're
not together!

It's natural and OK to miss your parents when you're not with them. Draw some of the things you'll do if you miss one of your parents.

My name is Annabelle, and I'm seven years old. My moms got divorced a few months ago. I wish they were still married. I miss all three of us being together and playing games or making cookies. When Mom is dropping me off at my house with Mama, I try to see if they're happy to be with each other. Sometimes I ask them if they can please get back together and try to be married again.

When parents are divorced, children often spend some of their time with one parent and some of their time with the other parent. Sometimes they miss being all together, like Annabelle does. But they also like having alone time with each parent. Draw a picture of something you like to do with each of your parents.

My moms explained to me that they aren't going to marry each other again, but they're still going to be a team to help take care of me and make sure I'm loved. They talk together about how I'm doing and what I need. I still have a family—it's just different than it used to be.

When parents divorce, a lot changes, but some things stay the same. Children still have parents who love them, other friends and family, school, and their favorite activities. Draw some of the things that will stay the same for you.

Hi! My name is José, and I'm eight years old. I love soccer and my dog, Patch. When my parents told me they were getting divorced, I was sad. But mostly I was worried about who would pick me up from soccer and who would take care of Patch. I knew I was going to miss Patch so much if I couldn't see him every day!

Do you have some worries like José about what will happen when your parents get divorced? Draw some of the things you're worried about.

I told my parents how worried I was, and they helped me make a calendar so I would know what days I was going to see Patch. They also told me they already made a plan and knew who was going to pick me up each day after soccer practice. Now there's a calendar at my mom's house and one at my dad's house too. So if I'm confused about my schedule, I can always look at the calendar where I am and know the plan.

What are some of the things you'd like to have on your calendar? You can write them or draw them here, and then ask your parents to help you write them on a calendar so you will know just what to expect.

MONDAY

TUESDAY

WEDNESDAY

THURSDAY

FRIDAY

SATURDAY

SUNDAY

Hello, I'm Taylor. My parents are divorced, and now I have two homes. My home with my dad is the house my parents used to live in together. My home with my mom is her new apartment. At first, I felt funny in our new apartment. I missed some of my toys from my house, and there were different sounds at night. I woke up a lot at night in my new room until I got used to everything.

When parents get divorced, lots of kids live in two homes. Maybe you do too. How has your home changed? Draw a picture of your home, or your two homes.

I'm getting used to having two homes now. My parents made sure I have some favorite clothes, toys, and games at both places. Now I can have fun, and my special things are with me wherever I am. I still take my most special stuffed elephant with me when I change houses, so I can sleep with him every night. I have a cozy bed to sleep in at both of my homes.

You probably have some toys that you like to play with no matter where you are. What toys or things do you like to keep at home? Draw some of the things you like to keep with you.

My name is Jin. This summer my parents got divorced, and now I'm starting second grade. I have a lot of questions. I wonder if anyone else in my class has divorced parents. I wonder what my friends will think about my family now that it's changed. Can I invite my friends over to both of my houses? Should I tell my friends that my parents got divorced?

Good friends are the ones we know will be kind to us and want to help us. Who are your good friends? They may be kids from your school, neighborhood, or activities. A good friend can also be a grown-up you know. Draw some of your good friends.

Guess what? I made a new friend in my class. His name is
José. José's parents are divorced too! I found out because
he told me he had one house with his mom and one with
his dad. I asked him if his parents were divorced, and he
said yes. I told him mine are too. José said he was worried
at first, but now he's happy because he spends time with
each of his parents.

Some children don't want to tell anyone about their parents' divorce, and some children want to tell everyone. It's best to choose good friends who you know really care about you to talk to about your family. Do you have a friend you'd like to tell about your parents' divorce? Draw a picture of yourself talking to them.

Hi, it's me, Sarah, again. It's almost my birthday. I'll be seven, and I'm really excited! But I'm also sad I won't be able to have cake on my birthday with both of my parents together. Now that they're divorced, they're each going to have their own time with me to celebrate my birthday. They're also both coming to my party with my friends. I wonder what that will be like.

When parents get divorced, birthdays and other celebrations are usually different from how they used to be. Sometimes divorced parents do things together, but usually children celebrate two times, once with each parent. Draw a picture of a celebration or other special time that will be different for you now.

My birthday was a lot different this year, but it was still really fun. My mom took me out to eat at my favorite restaurant on my birthday. Later that week, I had a delicious birthday cake with my dad. And they each gave me an awesome present! They both came to my party with my friends and watched me open my presents and play games. They even both met my friend Annabelle. She moved into my mom's neighborhood with her mom after her parents got divorced.

Draw what you would like your birthday to look like. Will you have a cake with candles or another special treat? Where will you celebrate your birthday? Who will be there?

Hi! I'm Avi, and I'm seven years old. My dads got divorced when I was only in preschool. I was so sad and confused, but I also didn't like hearing them argue. Now we're all feeling much happier. Sometimes my parents still disagree, but they work it out. I spend some weekends with my Dad and some with my Pop, and we can be peaceful and happy together. My grandma even moved in with my Dad!

Can you think of something that might be better or easier for you now that your family is changing? You can draw it here. If you can't think of anything yet, that's OK. Just leave this page blank and come back to it when you notice something is better for your family.

Sometimes I still feel sad about our family. Then I talk to my parents, my grandparents, or my counselor. Sometimes they can make a change in the schedule if I want extra time with one of my dads. If they can't, they still understand how I feel and have other ways to help. They remind me I'll see my other dad soon and give me a hug or help me make a card for him. This usually helps me feel better.

When parents divorce, children have lots of questions and feelings. Some of these questions and feelings come up when children first learn about the divorce, and others come later. Think about a feeling you wish your parents understood, and draw it here.

Hi there! It's Nate again. Even though I'm used to my parents being divorced, I still miss Mom when I'm with Dad, or miss Dad when I'm with Mom. But I know I can talk to them every night, and I can look at my calendar to know when I'll see them next. We have a schedule for everything, like who picks me up from school and who takes me to piano lessons. I know what to expect. When something changes, I figure it out with my parents' help.

Parents make a lot of decisions for their families. Families have plans for what they'll do on school days, weekends, and holidays. They may even have schedules for meals, bedtimes, and activities. Draw one of the plans your parents have made for you.

I've learned a lot about myself. It turns out I'm powerful and strong. I know how to pay attention to my feelings. I also talk about what I need, and I have ways to feel comforted and calm. When there's a problem, I can ask for help if I need it, and I can solve the problem. I'm so glad I have my parents to help me, and I've even learned how to help myself.

You have the power inside of you to listen to your feelings, talk about what you need, and solve problems. Draw a picture of some of the powers you know you have that will help you as your family changes.

What's Your Story?

Write the story of your changing family here.

_____

_____

_____

_____

_____

_____

_____

_____

_____

_____

_____

What Does Your Family Look Like?

Draw your changing family.

About the Author

Tracy McConaghie, LCSW, RPT/S, is a child and family therapist. She and her husband, Andrew, own McConaghie Counseling in Alpharetta, Georgia. Tracy specializes in divorce, childhood anxiety, and childhood behavior disorders. She also helps parents create their divorce parenting plan and resolve co-parenting challenges.

Tracy and Andrew have two adult children. Tracy enjoys reading, yoga, and baking in her free time.

About the Illustrator

Karen Greenberg is an NYC-based, self-taught illustrator with over 20 years of experience. Karen's award-winning illustrations have appeared in books, food and beverage packaging, CD covers, greeting cards, magazine pages, and more. Inspired by nature, Southern folk art, and all things mid-century, her self-taught style combines whimsy with a sophisticated take on the naive, and a strong design sensibility. In addition, Karen has been featured in *Becoming a Successful Illustrator* by Derek Brazell and *3x3* magazine's Showcase section, and has exhibited in The Bepo + Mimi projects gallery shows "Cut To The Drummer" and "First Signs of Spring."

Interior and Cover Designer: Lindsey Dekker
Art Producer: Janice Ackerman
Editor: Barbara J. Isenberg
Production Editor: Mia Moran
Illustration © 2020 Karen Greenberg

ISBN: Print 978-1-64611-521-1
R0

Printed in the USA
CPSIA information can be obtained
at www.ICGtesting.com
CBHW042048010524
7764CB00007B/113

9 781646 115211